Silk Ribbon Embroidery

A Workshop Approach for Beginners

HELEN DAFTER

SALLYMILNER
PUBLISHING

First published in 2007 by
Sally Milner Publishing Pty Ltd
734 Woodville Rd
BINDA NSW 2583
AUSTRALIA

© Helen Dafter 2007

Design: Anna Warren, Warren Ventures Pty Ltd
Editing: Anne Savage
Diagrams: Wendy Gorton
Photography: Tim Connolly

Printed in China

National Library of Australia Cataloguing-in-Publication data:

Dafter, Helen.
    Silk ribbon embroidery : a workshop approach for beginners.

    ISBN 9781863513678.

    1. Silk ribbon embroidery. 2. Handicraft. I. Title.
    (Series : Milner craft series).

    746.44704

10 9 8 7 6 5 4 3 2 1

Disclaimer
The information in this instruction book is presented in good faith. However, no
warranty is given, nor results guaranteed, nor is freedom from any patent to be
inferred. Since we have no control over the use of information contained in this
book, the publisher and the author disclaim liability for untoward results.

Contents

The projects **59**

Acknowledgements

I began embroidering when I was four years old under the watchful and often critical eye of my maternal grandmother. I am thankful for her patient tuition and the depth of knowledge she passed on. She did not teach me the needle art now known as Silk Ribbon Embroidery—in that I am completely self-taught—but the inherent skills and stitches that I had learned as a child formed a solid foundation when I eventually discovered and developed a passion for stitching with silk ribbons. I played with the silk ribbons I bought until I understood them and could stitch with them to my satisfaction—I then began a journey with the ribbons, taking them to places that others before me had not. Fellow embroiderers now recognise my simple style of embroidery with silk ribbon that is easily distinguished from others'. I take great satisfaction from that.

Since the establishment of my own embroidery business I am now in a position to talk to seasoned ribbon embroiderers and those who wish to take up this rewarding needle art on a regular basis. I have been in a unique position over the last twelve years, due to the hundreds of workshops conducted both in Australia and overseas, to gauge the interest level and the simple skills required to achieve success with this elegant and classic form of embroidery. Questions asked in workshops are often the same from one to another, and I have learned what information and skills need to be presented in an interesting and informative manner, with the appropriate diagrams and instructions, so that workshop participants can leave with both the knowledge and the confidence to try this needle art without structured classes or supervision by a qualified tutor.

In return may I say thank you to all those workshop participants and the many hundreds of students I have taught over the years and continue to teach—you have been the driving force behind this book. Without the opportunity to teach you and conduct workshops for you I would not have been forced to distil the information it contains. I trust you will find it useful.

I am also fortunate to have the generous support of talented and committed people in this industry. The task has been made easier because of you. A special thank you to Louise Howland from Rajmahal, a constant source of inspiration, support and a valued friend.

Once again my thanks are extended to my publishers for the opportunity to share skill and knowledge—their faith, their contribution and encouragement have been invaluable, once again an enjoyable experience.

And finally thank you, to my friends, my family and in particular my husband Glenn. In their own way they have been as patient and as constructively critical as my grandmother. They continue to give me the space, the support and the love. It makes all the difference.

Happy stitching.

Helen Dafter

Introduction

The art of using silk ribbon as an embroidery technique dates back to the early 17th century. Royal court garments, the military uniforms of high-ranking officers and the vestments and regalia of the clergy were decorated and richly embellished with silk ribbon embroidery. Later it was used by the French couture houses to set their unique and often costly garments apart with individual hand-embroidered embellishments on each one.

While silk ribbon embroidery has enjoyed varying degrees of popularity since those times, it was not until the late 20th century that it gained universal appeal and gained its deserved place as a recognised and widely practised form of embroidery.

Today this elegant needle art holds a significant place in the history of embroidery both in Australia and overseas. It is a much faster form of stitching than traditional cross-stitch or tapestry and its unique characteristics are ideally suited to the embellishment of garments and framed projects, as well as to the creation of useful and decorative objects for the home.

Often the simpler the design the more effective is the result. The most satisfying silk ribbon embroidery can be achieved with three or four simple stitches and a simple but elegant design.

The three flowers illustrated here—a daisy, a hydrangea and a foxglove—have been created using the same three stitches (stem stitch, French knot and ribbon stitch) and two different widths of ribbon. Effective design does not just mean knowing more stitches, it also means understanding where to put them to create an interesting embroidery.

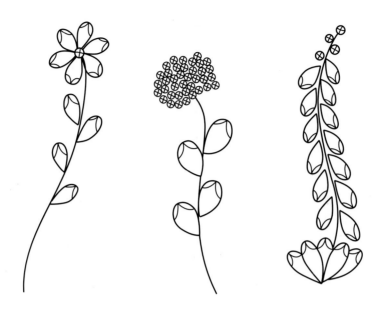

Three flowers made with the same three stitches used in different ways

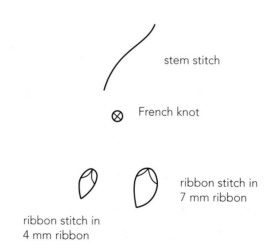

stem stitch

French knot

ribbon stitch in
7 mm ribbon

ribbon stitch in
4 mm ribbon

Materials and equipment

Silk ribbons

Silk embroidery ribbon is specifically designed and manufactured to be drawn through fabric using only a needle. It has woven edges but these are invisible. Ribbon is available in five different widths—2 mm, 4 mm, 7 mm, 13 mm and 32 mm. Approximately 185 plain dyed colours are available in the most commonly used width, 4 mm. The other four widths are not available in the same extensive colour range.

2 mm   4 mm   7 mm   13 mm

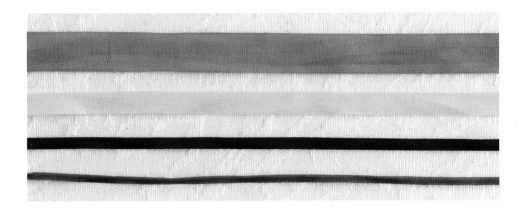

Specialty hand-dyed silk ribbon is becoming increasingly available. The colour of these ribbons varies along their length, shading from light to dark, and often with different complementary colours appearing as well. These hand-dyed ribbons are usually created by talented cottage industry artists and have good colour repeatability. A word of warning—the quantity of ribbon required for any project using hand-dyed ribbon should be purchased all at the one time as there may be subtle differences from one dye lot to the next. I find the wider hand-dyed ribbons, in particular the 7 mm ones, particularly useful as their changing tones and colours can bring an embroidery to life very quickly, delicately echoing the changing tones of flower petals and leaves.

Other types and widths of ribbon may be used for ribbon embroidery, with various effects achieved with the different materials. Two in particular are worthy of special mention.

Spark organdie A sheer organza ribbon, available once again in different widths, and very useful for subtle filling of background areas. It has an inherent sparkle which can be useful to lift areas of a design as well.

Spark organdie

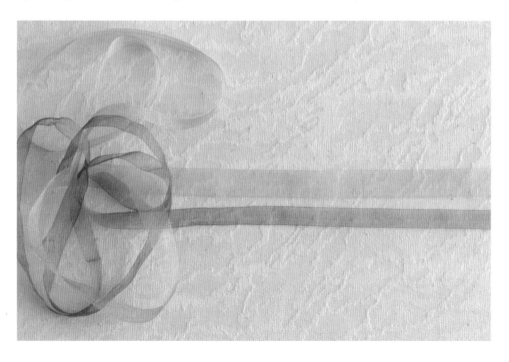

Hanah silk A bias width of silk fabric cut with a hot knife to ribbon width—9 mm, 16 mm, 25 mm and wider. It is hand-dyed. Due to the bias cutting of the 'ribbon' it frays easily when drawn through fabric but can give very interesting and dimensional effects when used in conjunction with more traditional silk ribbon embroidery techniques. Hanah silk can be used to create larger and more three-dimensional hand-formed flowers that can be sewn onto the surface of fabric rather than through it, as with traditional stitching.

From left:
9 mm,16 mm,
25 mm, 40 mm
hand-dyed
hanah silk

Ironing the ribbon

A newly purchased length of silk ribbon often needs to be ironed to remove creases and folds. Ironing will not damage it. The easiest method is to heat the iron, place the ribbon across a flat padded surface, ideally an ironing board, lower the sole of the iron onto the ribbon and quickly pull the length of ribbon under the iron. After pressing, the ribbon should be stored in such a manner that creases do not reoccur. Winding it around a ribbon storage spool is the best method of storage.

Ribbon storage
spool

Working length

The ideal length to cut when working with silk ribbon is 30 cm (12 in). Ribbon cut to this length will remain in good condition while you are working it; with a greater length you run the risk of wasting part of it due to ribbon fatigue, caused by being pulled back and forth through the fabric too many times.

Note Be wary of the imitation silk ribbons on the market. I do not use these ribbons as they do not create the same effect as real silk.

Needles, scissors and other sewing aids

Needles

The correct selection of size and type of needle used for silk ribbon embroidery is critical. With the right selection the ribbon will be drawn through the fabric easily and the edges will be protected. If you use the wrong size and type of needle, the ribbon will be difficult to draw through the fabric and the edges will become frayed and distressed, because the ribbon is suffering 'ribbon fatigue'.

The correct size and type of needle will force the fibres of whatever fabric you are working on far enough apart to allow the silk ribbon to be drawn through easily with minimum stress. Silk ribbon is strong, but it is also delicate and needs to be treated with respect.

Needle sizes are based on wire gauge size—the smaller the number the larger the needle.

Size 18 chenille needle This needle has a large eye, broad shaft and a sharp point, and is the needle most commonly used. It is used for 4 mm and 7 mm silk ribbons and for a broad range of finely woven/knitted fabrics such as silk, cotton and velvet.

Size 20/22 chenille needle These needles are smaller than the 18 but have the same attributes. They are useful for narrower 2 mm ribbon widths on the closely woven fabrics suggested above, or for use with 4 mm ribbons on more open-weave fabrics such as even-weave fabrics, linen, wool blanketing or wool doctor flannel, where the fibres of the fabric do not need to be pushed as far apart to allow easy passage of the silk.

Size 22 needle

13

Size 13 chenille needle A very large needle but indispensable when working with Hanah silk or some of the wider widths of silk ribbon.

Crewel 8 or 9 This is a general purpose hand-sewing needle with an elongated eye and a sharp point which I prefer when using stranded threads for detail stitching.

Note Needles are the embroiderer's most important 'hand tool'. With constant use or abuse they may become quite blunt. If a chenille needle, which normally has a sharp point, becomes blunt due to accidental damage or extended use, retire it and replace it with a new one. Alternatively, you can try sharpening it using a needle emery. Continued use of a blunt needle will result in ribbon fatigue and wastage.

Embroidery scissors

Always keep a very sharp pair of fine-pointed embroidery scissors close at hand as you work. Use them only for cutting

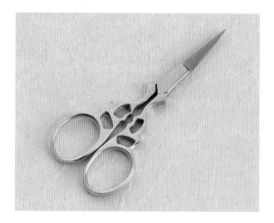

your stranded threads and silk ribbons to length. Never use them for paper or other materials as this will damage the blades and make it difficult to cut cleanly through ribbons and threads.

Fine-tipped water-erasable marking pen

A fine-tipped water-erasable pen is essential for marking designs on your fabric. Any marks visible when the embroidery is complete can be removed by gently dabbing them with a cotton bud (Q tip) that has been dipped in cold water, then allowing the fabric and ribbon to air dry. Some pens have quite thick tips, and the marks they make can be more difficult to remove. If you are in any doubt that the marks from the pen you intend to use may not be easily removed from the fabric you are working with, make a test mark on the edge or selvedge of the fabric and try removing it before marking out the entire design.

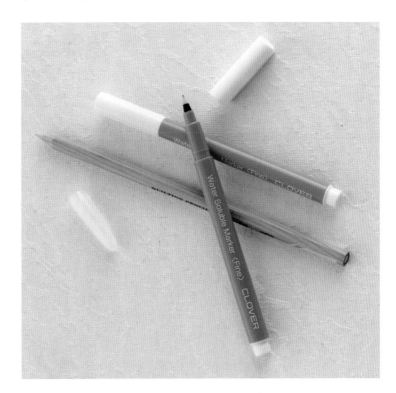

Embroidery hoop

A quality embroidery hoop which is easy to adjust and maintains tight even tension is essential. If the correct tension is kept on the fabric you are then free to concentrate on the tension and formation of your stitches and the fabric will not buckle, pull or crease as the stitches are formed. If possible, choose an embroidery hoop that will encompass the outer boundary of your embroidery surface. This will minimise 'bruising' or damaging completed stitches.

My preference is for the Susan Bates Super Grip Lip Hoop. The unique design of this plastic hoop maintains even tension on the fabric and eliminates the need to keep tugging the fabric to keep it taught. It is extremely lightweight and does not cause any wrist strain. If you are working on a square piece of fabric in a round embroidery hoop, use four safety pins in the corners of the fabric to pin the excess safely out of the way. This will

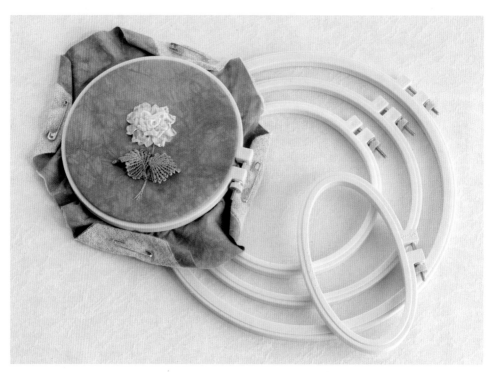

Embroidery hoops, interfacing, excess fabric folded to the back of hoop with safety pins in the corners

eliminate the risk of the excess fabric accidentally being sewn to the back of the work.

A 20 cm (8 in) embroidery hoop is an ideal size and my personal favourite to work with. If you are working on a smaller piece of precious fabric and only have a hoop of this size, strips of calico or cotton fabric can be sewn to the edges of the embroidery fabric so that it will 'fit' the hoop.

Pin/needle cushion

A pin/needle cushion kept close to where you are working is invaluable when working with silk ribbon. Mine holds a collection of chenille needles and crewel needles which are still threaded with the colours I have used on previous projects. By leaving the ribbon attached to the needle (see Locking On, under Getting Started) and using up the leftover ribbon prior to cutting a new length in the same colour I avoid wasting ribbon and get the maximum stitching from each length.

Needle cushion, showing the safe and effective storage of previously used lengths of silk ribbon.

Iron-on interfacing

A soft and flexible iron-on interfacing is a useful aid to making silk ribbon embroidery a little easier. I use it on all fabrics except wool blanketing or wool doctor flannel. The interfacing performs three tasks. Firstly, it stabilises a knitted fabric such as panne velvet, minimising the stretch and making it easier to embroider through. Secondly, it decreases the opacity of a light-coloured fabric—dark ribbons and threads are more difficult to see through the fabric, making it possible to jump short distances with less danger of 'shadowing' showing through to the front of the work. Thirdly, it allows you to bury the ends of the ribbon between the two layers of fabric to end off without having to secure the ends (see further note on Finishing Off). This is the greatest bonus of using interfacing, in that all the untidy ends left dangling as you change ribbons are buried between the layers, with the result that there is less opportunity to pull on them as you draw the needle through the fabric and thus damage existing stitching!

Fabrics

Unlike traditional cross-stitch, tapestry and other embroidery techniques requiring even-weave fabrics, silk ribbon embroidery allows many different types of fabric to be used. In fact, if the size 18 chenille needle can be drawn through a particular fabric quite easily, then that fabric can be used for silk ribbon embroidery. Obviously some fabrics are easier to use than others. Natural woven fabrics such as cotton, wool and silk are easy to work on, as are some polyester/cotton woven blends. Fabrics such as 100 per cent polyesters, knitted cotton and panne velvet are a little more challenging—if they are to be used for silk ribbon embroidery, an iron-on woven interfacing will make them much easier to work with, as the interfacing will stabilise the fabric and reduce the amount of 'stretch'.

When you are shopping for interesting and suitable fabrics to use as your embroidery background, consider some of the hand-dyed cotton fabrics primarily produced for the patchwork market. Some of these fabrics are produced with beautiful shading and a sense of movement which can imitate a natural background and in many cases reduce the need for a hand-painted background to help produce an interesting and realistic embroidery. Sumptuous fabrics such as silk velvet and silk habutae are also available hand-dyed from specialty suppliers. The combination of hand-dyed fabrics and silk ribbons is an elegant one.

The only fabrics which I would suggest are not suitable for ribbon embroidery are those that are sheer, such as chiffon, organza and similar fabrics. The weight of the embroidery tends to 'pull' these delicate fabrics, and because of their sheer nature it is difficult to hide the back of the embroidery and keep the front neat.

Note If you are still unsure if a fabric is suitable for silk ribbon embroidery, test it with a size 18 chenille needle. If the needle passes through the fabric easily then it is fine for your embroidery.

Stranded threads

Stranded threads of some type are usually necessary to complete a silk ribbon project. These are many and varied and personal preference will determine which is used.

For many years now I have preferred to work with Rajmahal stranded art silk, which I have found to be very sympathetic with silk ribbon. Both have an inherent lustre which stranded cotton thread lacks. Rajmahal thread is available in a range of 60 colours and comes in a 6-stranded skein 8 metres long. The scale of the work will determine how many strands are used but most work is done with either one or two strands. The colours I most commonly use are shades of green to embroider flower stems and detail stitching around flower buds. The colour of the stem is determined by matching as carefully as possible the thread to the colour of the ribbon used for the leaves. If the colours are too different, then a strand of one colour can be 'tweeded' with a strand of another to create a blended thread and thus match the silk ribbon more effectively. The size 8 or 9 crewel needle is used for these threads. Use the thread in short lengths only, approximately 50 cm (20 in), to minimise thread distress.

In some circumstances thicker threads may be required to achieve bulkier stitching. Multiple strands of a suitable stranded embroidery thread may be used or you may choose to source some of the hand-dyed specialty threads that are becoming more available.

The inherent lustre of Rajmahal threads in a variety of greens, worked either individually or 'tweeded', will be perfect for stems and detail stitching with silk ribbon embroidery.

General techniques

Getting started

Locking on

The technique of 'locking on' will prevent the silk ribbon falling out of the large eye of the chenille needle while you are working. It also allows you to work as much as possible of the cut length of the ribbon—only the last 5cm (2 in) will be lost. Remember to cut only a 30 cm (12 in) length to minimise ribbon fatigue.

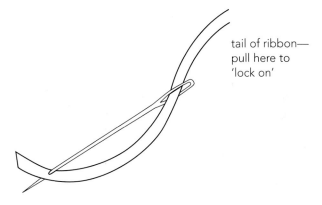

tail of ribbon—
pull here to
'lock on'

To lock the ribbon onto the needle, pass the end of the ribbon through the eye of the needle. Bring the threaded end of the ribbon up to the point of the needle and pierce the ribbon approximately 6 mm (¼ in) from the end. Pull this pierced end of the ribbon only *halfway* down the shaft of the needle. Hold the point of the needle between your thumb and forefinger and gently pull the other end of the ribbon (the tail) to complete the 'locking'.

Soft or loop knot

A quick and effective way to start working with a length of silk ribbon is to create a soft knot or loop which keeps the end of the silk ribbon at the back of the work. The loop so created lies quite flat against the back of the fabric without the bulk of a traditional knot.

stitch length approx. 6 mm (¼ in)

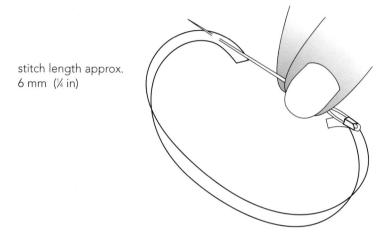

Lock the ribbon onto the chenille needle as described above. Hold the long end of the ribbon (the tail) between your thumb and forefinger with the length of ribbon draped away from you over your fingers. Pierce the end of the ribbon twice just above your thumb, approximately 6 mm (¼ in) apart with the point of the needle. This 6 mm stitch should be about 6–8 mm (⅜ in) from the end of the ribbon tail. Grasp the point of the needle and gently pull the needle through the ribbon where you have created this stitch. As you pull this through to the end of the ribbon a 'loop' will be created in the end of the ribbon which will form the 'soft knot'.

Note If you run your fingers down the length of ribbon beginning at the needle and fail to feel a 'bump' at the ribbon tail, then you have worked the stitch in the wrong direction with the needle pointed towards the end of the ribbon rather than away from it. Try again—this is a technique well worth acquiring for ease of starting.

Knotting stranded threads

A small neat knot at the end of each length of stranded thread is fine for starting—the small lump created will be minimal at the back of the work once silk ribbon is added.

Finishing off

How silk ribbon embroidery is finished off at the back of the work depends on what fabric you are working on, and on the ultimate use of the project. If the embroidery is going to be mounted and framed, it is not as important to finish things off as securely and neatly as it would be if it were a cushion, a blanket or some other item of heavy wear.

If you have used woven iron-on interfacing on a project which is not designed for active or heavy wear, then finishing off is often simple a matter of threading the ribbon or stranded thread beneath some of the existing stitching between the layers formed by the embroidery fabric and the interfacing, and snipping the end off neatly. This will keep the ends of the ribbon securely in place at the back of the work. I always turn the needle end for end and weave the eye rather than the point between the two layers, as this removes the risk of the needle point getting caught and pulling or damaging the work.

If the item is designed to receive heavy or active wear, or will need to be laundered, thread the silk ribbon between the layers, trim the end and, using a complementary coloured thread, sew the end of the ribbon at the back of the work to some of the existing stitching. On wool blanketing or wool flannel fabric where iron-on interfacing has not been used, simply thread the silk ribbon beneath the existing stitching and sew down, using the complimentary coloured thread. Be careful to hold the needle parallel to the fabric when threading beneath the stitching to avoid pulling the completed stitches on the front of the work.

Note Never attempt to tie a knot in the end of the silk ribbon you are finishing off, as this invariably results in pulled stitches!

Pattern transfer methods

Patterns can be transferred to your chosen embroidery fabric in a variety of ways. Experienced embroiderers often have a preferred method which may or may not be the same as those described here. I have, however, found these methods, although time consuming, to be foolproof.

Freehand transfer

This the simplest method, provided you have the confidence and do not mind that not all the design elements will be in the exact position shown on the design outline. Simply draw lines on the fabric using a water-erasable pen, and begin stitching.

Simple transfer method

If the fabric is quite sheer and pale in colour—silk, cotton, even in some cases wool doctor flannel—then quite often it is sufficient to place the design sheet beneath the fabric and simply trace over the major design elements only (see diagram below) using a water-erasable pen.

If you have difficulty seeing through the fabric, you can tape pattern and fabric together to a sunlit window, a computer screen, a glass-topped table with a strategic light source beneath it, or to a specifically designed light-box, to make the pattern easier to see and trace.

Design outline

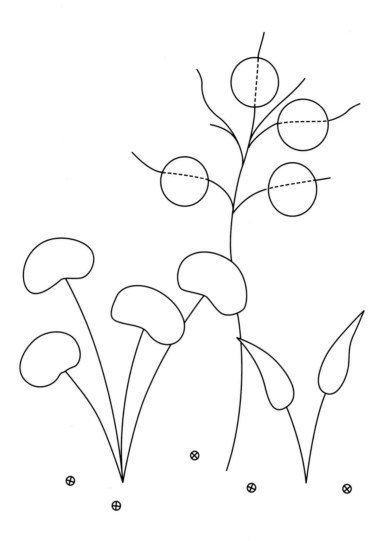

Design elements to be transferred—major stem lines, flower outlines, flower centres

Tulle transfer method

If your chosen embroidery fabric is too thick to see through using one of the methods described above, you may have to employ the tulle transfer method to accurately transfer the elements required.

Place a piece of non-waxed kitchen paper (lunch wrap) or tissue paper over your design sheet. Next, place a piece of fine bridal tulle or netting (available in fabric stores) over the tissue, and pin all three layers together to keep them in place. A permanent black fine-tipped laundry marking pen (available at newsagents) is then used to trace over the design elements to transfer the desired pattern to the tulle. Allow the pen marks to dry for several minutes. Remove the pins and discard the paper (which was only there to protect the original pattern sheet). Set the original pattern sheet aside.

Pin the tulle securely to your embroidery fabric and use a water-erasable fabric marking pen to trace over the lines made by the laundry marker. The fine holes in the tulle allow the tip of the marking pen to penetrate and thus mark the design elements onto your embroidery fabric.

If your fabric has a significant pile (for example, wool blanketing), hold the pen upright to allow maximum penetration of the tip through the tulle. If the marks are still difficult to see, you can carefully remove some of the pile in the design area using a razor before attempting to mark the design—but make sure you don't 'scalp' the blanketing.

The tulle transfer method is also very useful on dark fabrics which will not allow light to penetrate. A white pencil or a silver quilting pencil may be used to penetrate the tulle on black, dark green, navy blue or similar deep-coloured fabrics if you are unable to see the lines created by the water-erasable pen.

The piece of tulle is now permanently marked with this design, so you will be able to use it again, or perhaps use portions of the design on another project. You can also reverse the design by turning the tulle over.

Note Ensure that you do not use the laundry marking pen anywhere near your chosen piece of embroidery fabric, for you will not be able to remove any accidental marks.

Stitch glossary

Many of the stitches used with silk ribbon are traditional embroidery stitches. The one difference is ribbon stitch and its subtle variations.

The following is a comprehensive guide to the stranded thread and silk ribbon stitches I use to create simple and effective designs.

Stem stitch

This stitch is most often worked with stranded thread to create the stems and branches of the various flowers in a design.

Bring the needle up at A, reinsert at B and emerge at C.

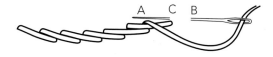

Repeat the process until the stem is the desired length and shape.

Hint To ensure the stitching follows a curved stem line, make sure the needle comes up on the *inside* of any curve along the line.

French knot

Often used with silk ribbon to create the centres of flowers or stitched in a group to create flower heads. Occasionally French knots in stranded thread may be used to add additional detail to a flower petal.

Draw the ribbon through the fabric from the back. With the needle point facing away from the fabric, wrap the silk around the needle once only. Stand the needle upright and put the point back into the fabric close to, but not in the same hole, where it emerged. Before pulling the needle and the ribbon through to the back of the fabric pull the ribbon gently but quite firmly around the shaft of the needle and ensure it sits close to the fabric. Pull the needle through to the back of the work. Proceed to the position of the next French knot required or fasten off.

Hint Keeping the same ribbon tension around the shaft of the needle will ensure that even sized French knots are created each time.

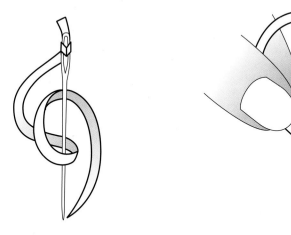

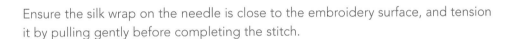

Ensure the silk wrap on the needle is close to the embroidery surface, and tension it by pulling gently before completing the stitch.

Ribbon stitch

The most commonly used stitch in ribbon embroidery, useful for creating petals, leaves and buds. There are several variations of this stitch.

Draw the ribbon through the fabric at the base of the stitch. Use the shaft of the needle as a tool at the base of the stitch, working it underneath the ribbon to encourage the ribbon to lie as flat as possible on the surface of the fabric. Put the point of the needle through the flattened ribbon 8–10 mm (⅜ in) from the start of the stitch and gently pull the ribbon back on itself until it forms a gentle petal-like point.

This stitch can be angled to the left or right by piercing the ribbon close to its left or right side, but most often is worked straight with the needle piercing the middle of the ribbon.

Note Avoid working this stitch too quickly or too tightly, because ribbon stitch is almost impossible to undo. If you think you may pull it too tight, place the tip of your finger over the ribbon so that it can't be pulled tight. If a ribbon stitch is accidentally pulled, see Camouflage or Waste Stitch (page 51).

Ribbon stitch with 4 mm ribbon

Extended ribbon stitch

Often worked in conjunction with basic ribbon stitch to create strap-like leaves and grasses. Commence the stitch in the same manner as ribbon stitch, determine the length required, then complete in the same manner as ribbon stitch.

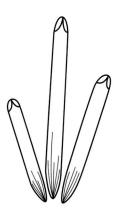

Extended and couched ribbon stitch

Used in a similar way as extended ribbon stitch, this variation has the added advantage of imitating strap-like foliage and leaves that bend over.

position of couching stitches

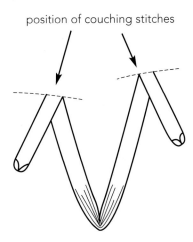

Commence the stitch in the same manner as for basic ribbon stitch, determine the length required to the fold line and hold the ribbon flat against the fabric. Take two or three small stitches in a complementary coloured stranded thread through the ribbon to 'couch' it in place on the surface of the fabric. Fold the ribbon over the stranded thread stitches to conceal them and then complete as detailed above.

Hint When you are working multiple extended and couched leaves in the same design, vary the angle of the bend to add visual interest.

Twisted ribbon stitch

A useful and easy stitch which allows you to create more interesting leaves and grasses. It is formed in the same way as traditional ribbon stitch, but the ribbon is allowed to twist one or more times before completing the stitch

Note Gives a very realistic effect to your stitching.

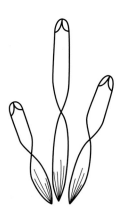

Straight stitch

This stitch can be worked in either stranded thread or silk ribbon. Using stranded thread, straight stitch is useful to create detail stitching on a flower petal, such as the face of a pansy, or the veins on a leaf. Worked in silk ribbon, straight stitch is often used to create leaves and add interest to backgrounds.

Note Pulling the silk ribbon tightly when creating a straight stitch allows you to work thinner leaves.

straight stitch formed with stranded thread

straight stitch formed with silk ribbon

Spider web woven rose

An easy technique combining two types of stitch that creates a realistic open rose. Using two strands of thread in the same colour as the ribbon chosen for the rose, begin with a double knot and work the foundation stitches of the rose using five even length and evenly spaced straight stitches. Anchor this thread off at the back of the work with a double knot. Draw the length of ribbon through the fabric close to the centre of one of the segments, and turn the needle several times until there are several twists in the ribbon. Reverse the needle and simply weave the eye of the needle with the ribbon attached under and over the spokes alternately. The first round should be pulled quite tight. Allow each subsequent round of woven ribbon to sit next to the one before it. Avoid pulling the ribbon too tightly on subsequent rounds as you weave the ribbon, as this will create a bulky rose and waste ribbon. If you have twisted the ribbon sufficiently the twists will form natural-looking petals as you weave. Return the ribbon to the back of the fabric once all the spokes are hidden, and fasten off.

Note Make sure that you fasten the stranded thread off with a double knot at the beginning and end of the foundation stitches; if they give way and pull through the fabric you will have to begin again.

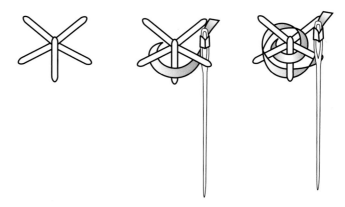

Weave the ribbon with the needle eye instead of the point to avoid catching the point in fabric or threads.

Fly stitch

This useful stitch is most commonly worked with stranded thread, and is often used for creating the detail stitching around a ribbon stitch to create a bud.

Draw the thread through fabric at A, insert at B and emerge at C, insert the needle through to the back of the fabric at D, the required distance below C.

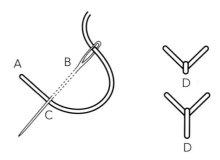

Bullion detached chain stitch

This stitch creates attractive buds and leaves or petals with a fine directional point and is very useful for creating native flowers, and the buds of flowers such as daffodils and roses.

Draw the ribbon through the fabric. Reinsert the needle next to the starting point but not in the same hole, then bring the point of the needle out at the length you want the stitch to be, usually 10–12 mm (⅜–½ in). Before pulling the needle through the fabric, wrap the silk ribbon once around the point of the needle, ensuring that it lies flat, with no creases around the shaft. Keep the tension on the ribbon at the base of the stitch with your thumb or finger tip, and gently pull the remainder of the needle shaft through the fabric and then the wrap of silk.

Lay the stitch on the fabric, determine which way it will lie best and then take the needle through the fabric immediately above the top edge of the wrap, taking care to angle the stitch in the desired direction.

Note This stitch can be lengthened a little by inserting the needle past the wrap in the final movement. This gives a fine point to the stitch and also allows it to be angled delicately.

wrap silk ribbon once around needle

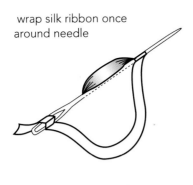

completing the stitch

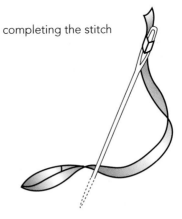

Gathered French knot flower

An extremely useful stitch which can be worked in a variety of ribbon widths to great effect in creating flower clusters or single flowers.

Draw the ribbon through the fabric, follow the directions for the formation of a French knot wrap around the needle above but ensure that the knot is firmly wrapped around the shaft of the needle approximately 2.5 cm (1 in) from the fabric surface. Pull the point of the needle back until it is just below the wrap of ribbon around the needle. Weave the point of the needle in and out of the 2.5 cm of ribbon between the wrap on the needle and the fabric surface—you should be able to take the needle in and out five or six times. Take the needle through the fabric next to where it came up and pull it through to the back. The gathers of ribbon will sit on the surface of the fabric with a neat French knot sitting in the middle.

Note Take care to make your gathering stitches even. This ensures that uneven loops of ribbon do not extend from the edge of the flower.

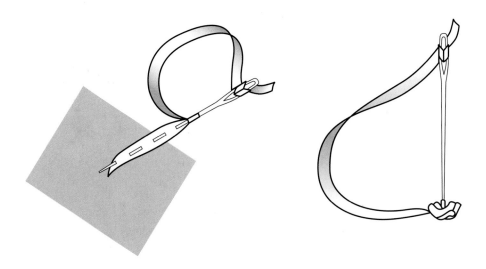

Full blown cabbage rose

This ribbon flower is created with a specific number of stitches sewn in a predetermined order.

The rose requires 11 stitches to complete. Following the diagram, work stitches 1 to 8 around a small oval space as shown. Stitches 1 to 6 are the same length, stitches 7 and 8 are shorter. Stitch 9 to 11 are worked in the order shown through the small oval left empty in the middle of petals 1 to 8. These last three stitches form the outer petals of the rose.

Note The cabbage rose is particularly impressive worked in 7 mm hand-dyed silk ribbon.

Loop stitch

Used to create dimensional petals or flower trumpets, this stitch is another variation of ribbon stitch. Draw the ribbon through the fabric and flatten as much as possible by running the shaft of the needle underneath the ribbon. If you wish to give the stitch more stability, make two or three small couching stitches in a complementary coloured stranded thread to catch the ribbon to the fabric. Loop the ribbon back over these stitches—don't put too much tension on it—and complete the stitch leaving the loop sitting proud of the surface.

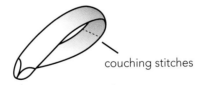

couching stitches

Note The tiny couching stitches are essential if loop stitch is used on an item to be worn, otherwise the loop can be very easily snagged.

Pistil stitch

A remote French knot with a 'tail' between fabric and knot. Using stranded threads this stitch is useful to create stamens and detail stitching in flower centres.

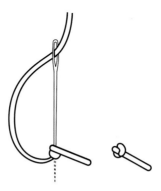

Detached chain stitch (lazy daisy)

Bring ribbon or thread through at A, take needle through the fabric at B, re-emerge at C and draw needle through fabric, ensuring the ribbon or thread is beneath the needle shaft. Take the needle down through the fabric over the thread or ribbon to fasten off. Position A and B as far apart as necessary.

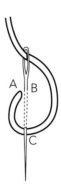

Partly open flower buds: combining stitches

Realistic flower buds can be worked with various combinations of ribbon stitch, fly stitch and straight stitch, as illustrated here. The shape of the particular bud required will dictate which combination you choose.

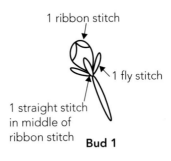

1 ribbon stitch

1 fly stitch

1 straight stitch in middle of ribbon stitch

Bud 1

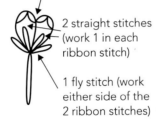

2 ribbon stitches

2 straight stitches (work 1 in each ribbon stitch)

1 fly stitch (work either side of the 2 ribbon stitches)

Bud 2

3 ribbon stitches

3 straight stitches (work 1 in each ribbon stitch)

1 fly stitch (work either side of the outer ribbon stitches)

Bud 3

Pointed flower bud: combining stitches

Long, pointed buds such as those of roses and daffodils are worked with a single bullion detached chain stitch combined with a fly stitch and several straight stitches.

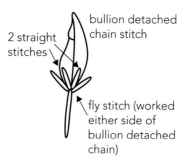

2 straight stitches

bullion detached chain stitch

fly stitch (worked either side of bullion detached chain)

Stitch legend

Symbols used in the designs for the projects.

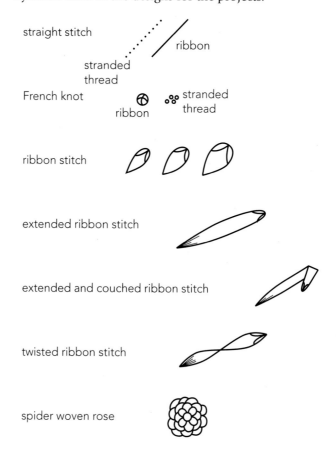

straight stitch

ribbon

stranded thread

French knot

ribbon

stranded thread

ribbon stitch

extended ribbon stitch

extended and couched ribbon stitch

twisted ribbon stitch

spider woven rose

bullion detached chain stitch

gathered French knot flower

full blown cabbage rose

fly stitch

loop stitch

pistil stitch

detached chain stitch

flower buds

pointed bud

Stitching and design techniques

Laying out the stitch

'Laying out the stitch' refers to the use of the chenille needle to manipulate the ribbon to keep it as flat as possible during the formation of ribbon stitch. This ensures the ribbon lies at its maximum width at the centre of each stitch. The needle shaft is narrower than the width of the ribbon, thus when the ribbon is drawn through the fabric it will be reduced in width and there will be folds at the edges. Use the shaft of the needle to encourage these folds to be as short as possible and to lie

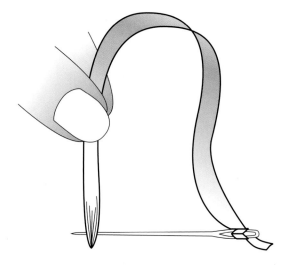

Using the needle to encourage the ribbon to lie flat.

underneath the ribbon when the stitch is completed. If the folds are facing up when the ribbon is pulled through the fabric, twist and turn the ribbon over, then use the needle shaft to gently lay the ribbon in place before piercing the middle of the ribbon to complete the stitch.

Note The ribbon can only be manipulated before the needle point pierces the ribbon to complete the stitch.

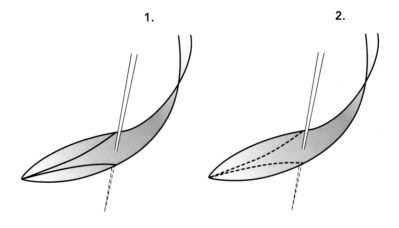

The folds in the ribbon, if any, should be on the underside, as shown in 2.

Order of work

In some instances the order in which you do the work in an embroidery is very important to reduce the risk of pulling existing stitches, or to create a dimensional appearance, or both.

For the daisy shown in this diagram, the order of work would be as follows: stem, flower centre, flower petals, leaves. By working the centre of the flower before the petals the risk of pulling the ribbon stitch petals is eliminated.

For the pansy, the stem is worked first, the centre second, the petals third, and the straight stitches of the pansy's face last, as once again this reduces the risk of pulling the ribbon stitches.

The straight stitches are worked from the outside of the petal towards the centre of the flower, as once again this reduces the risk of pulling these stitches.

Layering the flowers in the salvia spike is a commonsense approach based on the diagram you are following and isolating which flowers will need to be worked first. Work the stem first, the French knots next and the ribbon stitch last as the most economical way to complete this flower. The grasses and extended ribbon stitch behind the salvia spike should be completed before beginning the salvia spike.

Note In the project instructions the flower components are listed in the order in which they are to be worked.

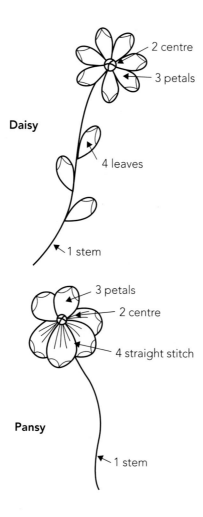

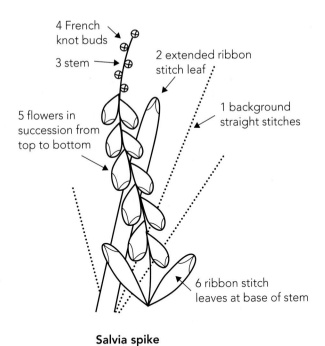

4 French knot buds

3 stem

2 extended ribbon stitch leaf

1 background straight stitches

5 flowers in succession from top to bottom

6 ribbon stitch leaves at base of stem

Salvia spike

Perspective stitching

Once you have mastered the basic stitches for ribbon embroidery it is a very simple matter to adjust the position and length of these stitches to create many varied and interesting looks for the flowers you embroider. By changing the position of the flower centre and by varying the length and position of the stitches that form the petals, a flower can be made to look as if

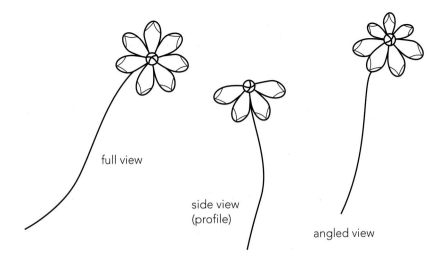

full view

side view (profile)

angled view

it is on its side and we are looking at a profile view, or from a different angle. This type of stitching is important in creating realistic effects in landscape or garden embroideries.

Note Any detail stitching on the flower petals with stranded thread will need to follow the ribbon stitches so that the detail stitches do not disturb the perspective created.

Scale: increasing and decreasing

Sometimes a flower or a leaf needs to be made larger or smaller for design reasons. But simply to make a ribbon stitch longer to increase the size of a daisy, for example, is going to compromise the scale of the flower so that it appears 'wrong' in the overall design. If a design element needs to be increased or decreased in size, the width of the ribbon you are using should be adjusted as well. This diagram shows the same flower design as it appears in different ribbon widths.

4 mm ribbon

7 mm ribbon

Economical use of silk ribbon

Silk is an expensive fibre, some say the queen of fibres, so you need to develop techniques which ensure that your ribbons are used in the most economical way so that your collection goes further and allows you to work more projects.

Leaving every working piece of silk ribbon attached to a

needle until it is completely used up will ensure that there is no wastage of ribbon (see notes under Pin/Needle Cushion).

Working ribbon embroidery stitches, particularly ribbon stitch itself, in a certain order can make an enormous difference to the amount of ribbon which is visible as stitches on the front of the work and the amount of ribbon 'wasted' in jumping from one stitch to the next at the back of the work. Sensible stitching regimes can achieve this with minimal waste. Illustrated here are two flower design diagrams which show the position of the stitches on the front of the fabric and show as a dotted line the path of the ribbon at the rear of the fabric from one stitch to the next. The first diagram illustrates the most economical path to use as the leaves are embroidered, moving upwards from leaf 1 to leaf 4. The second diagram shows the extra ribbon used when the stitches are started at the other end of the stem. Always consider the most economical stitching path before you commence your embroidery.

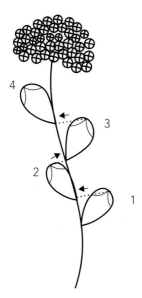

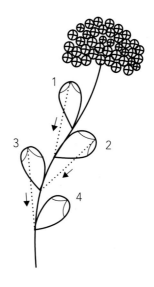

economical use of ribbon

wasteful use of ribbon

To jump or not to jump

A commonsense approach is required when deciding whether to jump across the back of the work to the next flower or stitch which requires the ribbon or thread you are currently using. Ask yourself these questions:

1   Will the stranded thread or ribbon be visible through the fabric from the front of the work? If shadowing will occur, do not carry the thread or ribbon but finish off and start again.

2   Will you use more ribbon by finishing off and starting again or will it be more economical to jump a short distance to the next flower or stitch? Always work as economically as possible.

3   Is there any danger of the ribbon strung across the back of the work being accidentally caught as you stitch? Keeping the back of your work neat means there is less likelihood of pulling existing stitches.

4   What is the ultimate use of the item? Large loops at the back of the work are a recipe for disaster on a heavy wear item.

Keep these points in mind as you stitch and jump to achieve neat, tidy and economical stitching.

Perfect petal placement

Achieving evenly spaced petals every time on simple flowers such as daisies and forget-me-nots comes with practice, but until that skill is acquired keeping a few simple techniques in mind as you stitch will make it easier.

Using a water-erasable pen, draw a line on the fabric to represent the middle of each petal. If the petal is to be worked with a simple ribbon stitch this mark needs only to be a straight line to represent the length and position of the stitch required.

To get all the petals the same length, try drawing a circle around the flower centre using a coin or a clear plastic circle of the required size as a template. Mark the flower centre in the middle. Lay down ribbon stitches of even length around the flower centre, extending to the circle drawn on the fabric. Providing the flower centre is in the middle of the circle all the petals will be the same length.

petals of even length

This same technique can be used when embroidering flowers with perspective—simply offset the flower centre and work petals to the circle edge.

flower with offset centre,
uneven length petals

Flowers with five petals Mark the fabric with a Y, then draw in two more lines to complete the five evenly spaced spokes.

Flowers with six evenly spaced petals Mark the fabric with three intersecting fine lines—from 12 o'clock to 6 o'clock, from 2 o'clock to 8 o'clock, and from 4 o'clock to 10 o'clock.

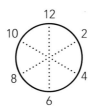

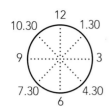

Flowers with eight evenly spaced petals Mark the fabric with four intersecting fine lines—from 12 o'clock to 6 o'clock, from 1.30 to 7.30, from 3 o'clock to 9 o'clock, and from 4.30 to 10.30.

If more petals than eight are required, generally the flower centre will be created using more than one French knot, most likely a cluster, and the width of the ribbon will determine the number of petals. Simply work the flower petals as evenly as possible, spacing them by eye as you go.

Note The fewer petals a flower has the shorter the stitches need to be, otherwise the flower may start to resemble a propeller, as illustrated by this diagram.

propeller-like, unbalanced

balanced

Colour selection

Putting a working combination of colours together for a pleasing effect is often a confusing and difficult task for embroiderers who are just starting out with innovative and original designs. The use of colour is a very subjective matter, and even colours which you do not necessarily like may need to be included in a design to give the embroidery integrity and balance. If you lack colour confidence or need a starting point, you may find that one or more of the following ideas will give you assistance and encouragement.

1   Take a colour photograph of a small scene or a plant in your garden to base your design on. Alternatively, find a picture that appeals in a book or magazine and use that.

2   Embroider from nature—select plants from your garden or a friend's garden which are easily interpreted in silk ribbon embroidery and a combination of simple stitches.

3   Use garden, bulb or seed catalogues—these are a valuable resource for different plant types and in particular for the different colours that many plants display.

4   Find a fabric that appeals to you just because of its colours—ignore the pattern and the design and use the fabric's colour combination as a visual cue to help you select the ribbons to use in your own creative embroidery design.

5   Work safely—when you are starting out, stick to a limited palette; gradually, as your design skills increase, add more colours.

Note For a design to be realistic the following hint may prove helpful—always include a shade or tone of purple/mauve to give the design depth and mood, and shades of lemon/yellow to give it lightness and interest. The inclusion of just a small amount of these two colours will increase the realism of any multicoloured embroidery project.

Camouflage or waste stitch

This is one of the most useful stitching techniques to keep in mind as you work, particularly until you get a feel for the correct tension required for the various stitches and understand manipulation of the ribbon to get it to sit flat on the fabric.

A camouflage or waste stitch is required if you accidentally 'pull' the end of the ribbon stitch you are creating through to the back of the fabric. Because the formation of a ribbon stitch requires you to pull the ribbon back through itself it is almost impossible to undo—and it leaves a large hole in the ribbon if you do manage to undo it. Rather than cutting the stitch out, having to sew down the cut end near the previous stitch and re-knot your ribbon, it is easier to create a camouflage stitch to disguise the stitch that has been pulled. Simply tension the pulled stitch as much as possible to make the ribbon thinner, and work a perfectly formed ribbon stitch straight over the top of the tensioned one. This will cover the stitch, is less wasteful of ribbon and allows you to move quickly on to the next stitch.

Background techniques

Painted backgrounds

Painting simple cotton or silk backgrounds to create dimensional embroidery backgrounds was how I first became interested in using these techniques to increase the amount of perspective a piece displays. Simple one-colour backgrounds can increase the amount of depth and visual interest of any embroidery. These days, more often than not, I pre-paint a fabric before embroidering a design, even though it may not be a design for a 'garden landscape'. Painting the background is often listed as an optional touch in embroidery instructions but it does give you an

opportunity to create a sense of perspective before threading a needle. The technique works very well with flowers, foliage or shrubs, which all lend themselves to perspective stitching.

Below are a number of helpful hints which you should keep in mind when pre-painting fabric for embroidery.

1   If possible, always work on dry unwashed fabric.

2   Many fabrics are suitable to 'paint' but there are subtle differences between them. Cotton such as natural homespun is a personal favourite and probably the easiest to use.

3   Acrylic fabric paint is used to create the background for the designs. (If this is difficult to obtain you can use folk art paint mixed with a textile medium.) The four colours which I most often use include two shades of green, a foliage green and a darker green for highlights, a light cream and a deeper caramel colour, which is useful for paths and rockeries. I supplement this basic palette with a soft grey and a light blue when creating more complex designs.

4   If the item you are pre-painting is designed for use and will need washing, check whether the paint you are using needs to be ironed to 'set' it. Always follow the manufacturer's instructions.

5   Inexpensive bristle brushes are effective for applying the paint, as are small soft sea sponges.

6   Before application, always dilute the paint to the lightest shade you require. More paint can always be added to increase depth of colour, but paint is almost impossible to remove if applied too heavily in the first instance. A ratio of 1 part paint to 9 parts water (at the most 2 parts paint to 8 parts water) is recommended to start with. When this has been applied to the fabric, stronger highlights of the same colour or a darker shade can be added by applying a little more to the areas where it is required.

7   A scrap of the fabric you intend to use is always handy to have close at hand so that you can try the shade before applying it to the working fabric.

8   A hair-dryer is a handy tool during the painting process as it can be used to speed up the drying time, particularly between the application of different colours. It can also be useful to spot dry areas where too much water has been applied.

9   Always dry a completed area before applying another colour to minimise bleeding.

10   If you do happen to apply an area of colour in a deeper shade than you would have liked to begin with, don't try to remove it or water it down—you will just make a mess. Finish the remainder of the painted background and later on you can embroider over the mistake to camouflage it. Chances are any small mistakes in the background can be covered with ribbon embroidery (it is very forgiving) and you will be the only one who knows. You can also disguise small areas where one colour has bled into another by strategically placing suitable flowers over the questionable spots.

11   Always keep in mind that you are simply creating a background to embroider over. The painted background does not need to be complicated or a dominant feature. It will become an integral part of the work but not the most important part—that should always be the hand embroidery.

Jacquard, hand-dyed cotton, hand-dyed silk velvet, hand-dyed silk habitae and iron-on interfacing.

Hand-dyed fabric backgounds

If you still a little reluctant to create your own background, an alternative is to make use of commercially available hand-dyed fabrics. Many talented craftspeople make these types of fabric, which are commercially available. They can bring an acceptable level of realism to your work without creating a background yourself.

Embellishment with silk ribbon embroidery

The opulent nature of silk embroidery ribbon lends itself to the sumptuous embellishment of all manner of items. It can become a very dimensional type of embroidery if hand-formed flowers are included among the stitched embroidery. These can be created using traditional silk ribbons, although more often than not they are created using bias-cut hand-dyed silk cut to a 'ribbon', up to 40 mm (1½ in) wide.

Hand-dyed laces, leaf motifs, beads and semiprecious stones can further add to this technique. It can lead to rich and fanciful works.

Project 3 uses this technique to create a rich spray of flowers to embellish the surface of an elegant evening bag.

Today's easy access to computers and advanced printing techniques allows pictures, drawings and other forms of design to be repetitiously printed on various fabrics (including cotton, silk and other natural fibres, and artificial fibres). These prints give infinite embellishment possibilities. Silk ribbon is a natural choice to embellish these fabric pictures in combination with stranded threads, beads and so on.

Note If you are planning to transfer to fabric a picture or print, either yourself or by paying to have it done for you, please ensure that this does not breach any copyright that may be held on the image.

Silk ribbon has also been used for many years to embellish

'crazy patchwork', as its dimensional nature covers the seams of the patchwork quickly and effectively.

Innovative stitching can be used with crazy patchwork, as silk ribbons can be used in combination with other threads to create unique results. In this situation the stitches do not have to create realistic floral components but simply add interest and further embellish the work.

Note Choose your stitches carefully for any embellishment on quilts and similar items to avoid delicate stitches being pulled during everyday use.

Problem solving: FAQs

1   *My stitches don't look like yours—I seem to pull them too tightly,. What am I doing wrong?*

Tension, particularly of ribbon stitch, is the single biggest technique to master when you begin to work with silk ribbon. Ensure you are working in a hoop to keep even, tight tension on the fabric. If you are still tensioning the stitch too tightly as you pull the ribbon through to the back of the work, try placing your finger nail or your finger tip at the end of the stitch to prevent it being pulled through too far as you gently pull the

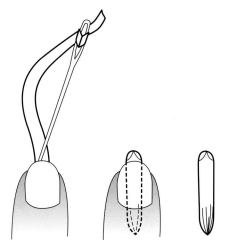

Anchoring a ribbon stitch with a finger tip to prevent pulling it too tight.

ribbon through to the back. Slow down! Stitches are often pulled if you work too quickly and do not take the time to lay the stitch out or to form the stitch correctly.

2 *My ribbon starts to fray and ladders up the middle. How can I prevent this?*

Check your needle size and also remember to only work with a maximum length of 30 cm (12 in) of ribbon. This will ensure minimum ribbon distress as you stitch.

3 *What type of fabrics can I use?*

Check if the chenille needle will pass easily through the fabric. If it does then you should be able to stitch through it. Refer to Fabric Selection.

4 *If I pull a ribbon stitch too tight can I undo it?*

The formation of a ribbon stitch makes it difficult to undo, and even if you do get it undone there will be a hole where the ribbon passed through itself. It is much easier to pull the offending stitch even tighter and camouflage it with a waste stitch. Refer to Stitching and Design Techniques.

5 *Do I need always to work in an embroidery hoop?*

When tension is evenly maintained on your embroidery fabric by using a hoop, it is much easier to concentrate on the tension of your stitching and there is less likelihood of pulled stitches. Hoops are quite easy to master and you will see an improvement in your stitching.

6 *How do I avoid pulling stitches when I need to stitch flower stamens or detail stitching?*

If the flower has a lot of overlapping petals, work the detail stitches back towards the centre of the flower to minimise the risk of pulling the stitches. Stamens created using pistil stitch will often pull ribbon stitch. If this is the case, try creating the stamens with a straight stitch to the centre of the flower and then adding a French knot for the pollen at the end of the straight stitch.

7   *How far can I jump at the back of the work with my silk ribbon?*

This will depend on the colour of the ribbon being used, the colour of the fabric, the ultimate use of the item and how economical you wish to be with the silk ribbon. See Stitching and Design Techniques.

8   *Can I wash my silk ribbon embroidery?*

Yes, silk is a natural fibre and can be washed when necessary. Take due care, hand-wash with a mild detergent, and dry flat. Avoid the use of stain removers, particularly with hand-dyed ribbons.

If the item requires ironing, place it embroidered side down on a clean towel, and press as necessary, avoiding the embroidered area. If the embroidery becomes flattened, spray it with clean water using an atomiser or laundry sprayer. The ribbon embroidery will sit up and restore itself.

9   *My stem stitch does not follow the curved stem line I have drawn. Why not?*

If you keep the needle on the same side of the stitching and on the inside of any curve you will achieve very neat stem stitching. This may mean swapping sides if a stem is a lazy S shape. You may know this stitching technique as 'thread up/thread down'.

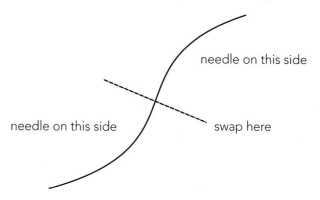

needle on this side

needle on this side

swap here

The Projects

Each of these projects has been carefully thought out to give you experience with the widest variety of stitches possible, and graded from beginner through to advanced. Interesting fabrics and applications for the embroidery have been included in the projects, as well as a hand-painted background for the advanced project.

It is important to work the flower components in the order listed for each project. This ensures dimension is built up during the embroidery process and will minimise damage to existing stitching when detail stitches and flower centres are created.

Note While I have specified Helen Dafter silk ribbons in these projects, the colour numbers used are standard and other brands of silk ribbon can be substituted if necessary. Colour Streams and Glenlorin ribbons are specific requirements.

PROJECT 1:
Four embroidered handtowels with native and cottage flowers

PROJECT LEVEL: BEGINNER

Flannel flowers

Stitches used

Stem stitch, French knots, bullion detached chain stitch, ribbon stitch, straight stitch (stranded thread).

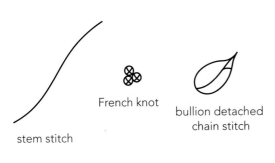

French knot

bullion detached chain stitch

stem stitch

ribbon stitch

straight stitch (stranded thread)

Requirements

hand towel (commercially available)

25 x 60 cm (10 x 24 in) toning cotton fabric to create embroidered border (this amount ensures sufficient fabric to fit in the hoop and also fits a range of hand towel sizes)

iron-on interfacing

Rajmahal stranded art silk 805

4 mm Helen Dafter silk ribbon:

  1 m x colour 62

  1 m x colour 33

  1.5 m x colour 1

no. 9 crewel needle for use with stranded threads

no. 18 chenille for use with silk ribbons

water-erasable pen

20 cm (8 in) embroidery hoop

Method

Transfer the design to the centre of the fabric band (leave the fabric larger if possible to allow it to be fitted in an embroidery hoop). Following the order of work below, complete the embroidery. Remove any marks made by the water-erasable pen. Turn under a 1 cm (⅝ in) seam allowance all round and using a toning thread stitch the embroidered border in place on the hand towel.

Tracing outline

Order of work

Stems: 2 strands Rajmahal 805; stem stitch

Flower centres: 4 mm ribbon x colour 62; one-wrap French knot

Flower petals: 4 mm ribbon x colour 3; bullion detached chain stitch

Leaves: 4 mm ribbon x colour 33; ribbon stitch

Leaf detail: 1 strand Rajmahal 805; straight stitch

Roses

Stitches used

Stem stitch, spider web woven rose, bullion detached chain stitch, ribbon stitch, straight stitch (stranded thread)

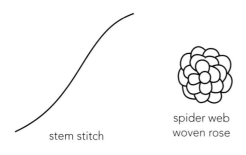

stem stitch

spider web woven rose

ribbon stitch

bullion detached chain stitch

straight stitch (stranded thread)

Requirements

hand towel (commercially available)

25 x 60 cm (10 x 24 in) toning cotton fabric to create embroidered border

iron-on interfacing

Rajmahal stranded art silk 521

4 mm Helen Dafter silk ribbon:

  1 m x colour 20

  2 m x colour 163

no. 9 crewel needle for use with stranded threads

no. 18 chenille for use with silk ribbons

water-erasable pen

20 cm (8 in) embroidery hoop

Method

Transfer the design to the centre of the fabric band (leave the fabric larger if possible to allow it to be fitted in an embroidery hoop). Following the order of work below, complete the embroidery. Remove any marks made by the water-erasable pen. Turn under a 1 cm (⅝ in) seam allowance all round and using a toning thread stitch the embroidered border in place on the hand towel.

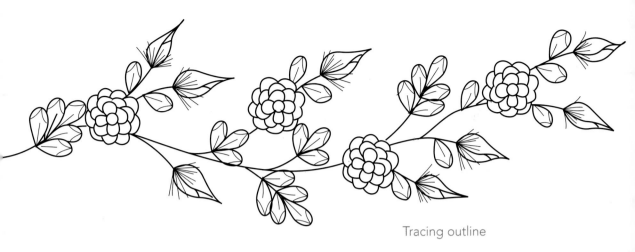

Tracing outline

Order of work

Stems: 2 strands Rajmahal 521; stem stitch

Roses: 4 mm ribbon x colour 163; spider web woven rose

Rose buds: 4 mm ribbon x colour 163; bullion detached chain stitch

Bud calyx: 2 strands Rajmahal 521; straight stitch

Leaves: 4 mm ribbon x colour 20; ribbon stitch

Leaf detail: 1 strand Rajmahal 521; straight stitch straight stitch

Callistemon

Stitches used

Stem stitch, French knots (ribbon and thread), gathered French knot flower, straight stitch (ribbon)

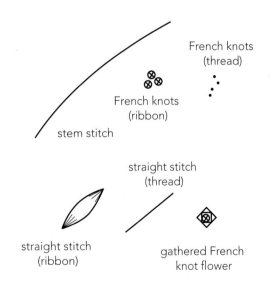

French knots
(thread)

French knots
(ribbon)

stem stitch

straight stitch
(thread)

straight stitch
(ribbon)

gathered French
knot flower

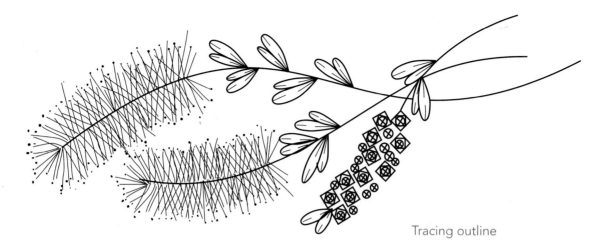

Tracing outline

Requirements

hand towel (commercially available)

25 x 60 cm (10 x 24 in) toning cotton fabric
    to create embroidered border

iron-on interfacing

Rajmahal stranded art silk: colours 171, 45,
    256

4 mm Helen Dafter silk ribbon:
    1 m x colour 52
    1 m x colour 72

no. 9 crewel needle for use with stranded
    threads

no. 18 chenille for use with silk ribbons

water-erasable pen

20 cm (8 in) embroidery hoop

Method

Transfer the design to the centre of the fabric
band (leave the fabric larger if possible to
allow it to be fitted in an embroidery hoop).
Following the order of work below, complete
the embroidery. Remove any marks made by
the water-erasable pen. Turn under a 1 cm
(⅝ in) seam allowance all round and using a
toning thread stitch the embroidered border
in place on the hand towel.

Order of work

Stems: 2 strands Rajmahal 171; stem stitch

Callistemon 'petals': 1 strand Rajmahal 256;
    straight stitch

Flower pollen: 2 strands Rajmahal 45;
    French knot

Seed pods: 4 mm ribbon x colour 52;
    gathered French knot, French knot

Leaves: 4 mm ribbon x colour 72; straight
    stitch

Daisies

Stitches used

*Stem stitch, French knot (stranded thread),
ribbon stitch, straight stitch (stranded thread)*

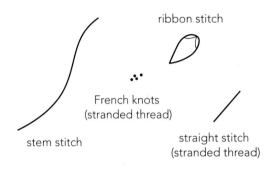

Requirements

hand towel (commercially available)

25 x 60 cm (10 x 24 in) toning cotton fabric
  to create embroidered border

iron-on interfacing

Rajmahal stranded art silk 521, 45

4 mm Helen Dafter silk ribbon:

  1 m x colour 20

  2 m x colour 13

no. 9 crewel needle for use with stranded
  threads

no. 18 chenille for use with silk ribbons

water-erasable pen

20 cm (8 in) embroidery hoop

Method

Transfer the design to the centre of the fabric
band (leave the fabric larger if possible to
allow it to be fitted in an embroidery hoop).
Following the order of work below, complete
the embroidery. Remove any marks made by
the water-erasable pen. Turn under a 1 cm
(⅜ in) seam allowance all round and using a
toning thread stitch the embroidered border
in place on the hand towel.

Order of work

Stems: 2 strands Rajmahal 521; stem stitch

Flower centres: 2 strands Rajmahal 45;
  French knots

Flower petals: 4 mm ribbon x colour 13;
  ribbon stitch

Flower detail: 1 strand Rajmahal 45; straight
  stitch

Leaves: 4 mm ribbon x colour 20; ribbon
  stitch

Tracing outline

PROJECT 2:
Lidded box with penstemons and daisies

PROJECT LEVEL: INTERMEDIATE

Stitches used

Straight stitch (stranded thread and ribbon), stem stitch, ribbon stitch, extended ribbon stitch, twisted ribbon stitch, French knots (thread and ribbon)

Requirements

25 cm (10 in) square of hand-dyed cotton fabric, dark moss green

25 cm (10 in) square of iron-on interfacing (optional, but recommended)

Rajmahal art silk: colours 421, 65, 805, 311, 45, 29

2 mm Helen Dafter silk ribbon: 2 m x colour 1

4 mm x 3 m Colour Streams hand-dyed 'Dusk' silk ribbon:

4 mm Helen Dafter silk ribbon:

1 m x colour 33

1 m x colour 171

1 m x colour 20

1 m x colour 75

1 m x colour 21

Tracing outline

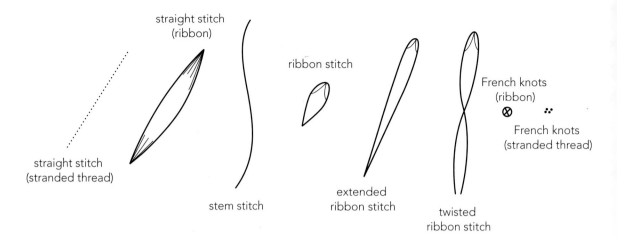

straight stitch
(ribbon)

ribbon stitch

French knots
(ribbon)

French knots
(stranded thread)

straight stitch
(stranded thread)

stem stitch

extended
ribbon stitch

twisted
ribbon stitch

1 black seed bead

Rajmahal hand-sew metallic thread: silver

no. 9 crewel needle for use with stranded
   threads

no. 18 chenille for use with silk ribbons

20 cm (8 in) embroidery hoop

water-erasable pen

Preparation

Trace the design outline and the major stems, leaves, etc. onto the fabric with the water-erasable pen. Fuse the interfacing to the back of the fabric. Tension the fabric in the embroidery hoop until it is drum tight.

Note Because of the crowded nature of this embroidery, it is important to work the elements in the order given, referring to the step-by-step diagrams as you go. Some stitches may need to be threaded beneath existing stitches to create the dimensional effect. The colours for the grasses and leaves can be varied a little if you prefer.

Method

Background grasses: 2 strands of Rajmahal 421, 805, 311, 65 separately; work long and short stitches across the design.

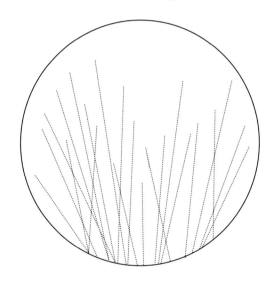

Guide to placement of background grasses

Grasses: 4 mm ribbon 20, 75, 33, 171 separately; work extended straight stitch, ribbon stitch and twisted ribbon stitch across the design. (Work bottom to top, top to bottom with each colour to ensure economy of ribbon usage.)

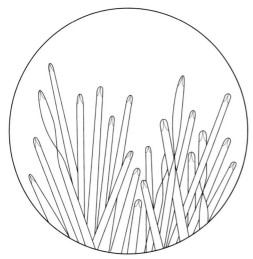

Guide to placement of silk ribbon grasses

Penstemon spikes: Using 2 strands of Rajmahal 805 work gently curving stems over existing embroidery in stem stitch. Flowers are worked in 4 mm 'Dusk', starting at the top of each stem with three or four French knots either side, and then working ribbon stitch down the stem. The short leaves at the base of the flower spike are formed with 4 mm ribbon, colour 33, as straight stitches pulled tight up the stem

Daisies: Using the photograph or the tracing outline as a guide, with 2 strands of Rajmahal 45 work a series of single-wrap French knots until the centre of each flower has been formed—a circle of knots for the two full flowers and an oval for the five flowers in profile. Using 2 mm ribbon in colour 1, work the petals in ribbon stitch and twisted ribbon stitch, overlapping as necessary to get a full effect. Where the stems are visible below the flowers, work them in stem stitch, 2 strands colour 65. Leaves are worked in straight stitch, 4 mm ribbon in colour 21.

Using the photograph as a guide, embroider the spider web in the metallic silver thread, making straight stitches for the spokes first, then filling in the web with straight stitch. Sew the seed bead in place using 4 straight stitches of a single strand of Rajmahal 29 through the bead, extending each side to form the eight legs.

Finishing

Remove any visible marks left by the water-erasable pen with a cotton bud dipped in cold water. Mount as a lidded box cover or frame the work if you prefer.

Guide to placement of penstemon spikes

PROJECT 3:
Embellished evening bag

PROJECT LEVEL: INTERMEDIATE

This elegant evening bag uses gathered and fringed Hanah silk to create the floral centrepiece of a fantasy design which uses the fabric colours to cue the colours of the finished design. Delicate hand-dyed lace leaves, flowers and beads add further interest. This design could easily be adapted to embellish crazy patchwork if you like.

Tracing outline

Finished size of bag: 18 x 22 cm

Stitches used

Hanah silk (fringed and gathered), stem stitch, gathered French knot flower, bullion detached chain stitch, French knot, spider web woven rose, simple beading techniques

Requirements

20 x 46 cm chosen fabric; leave larger if possible to allow fitting into the embroidery hoop (can be trimmed to correct size later); additional fabric will be needed if a pocket is made on the back of the bag

18 x 22 cm iron-on interfacing

Rajmahal art silk 805

50 x 25 mm Hanah silk 'Victorian Rose'

4 mm Colour Streams silk ribbon: 6 m x colour 'Berry'

4 mm Helen Dafter silk ribbon: 3 m x colour 75

burgundy seed beads #11

matt gold pearls 3 mm

hand-dyed lace leaves and flowers (ribbon embroidery could be substituted for these)

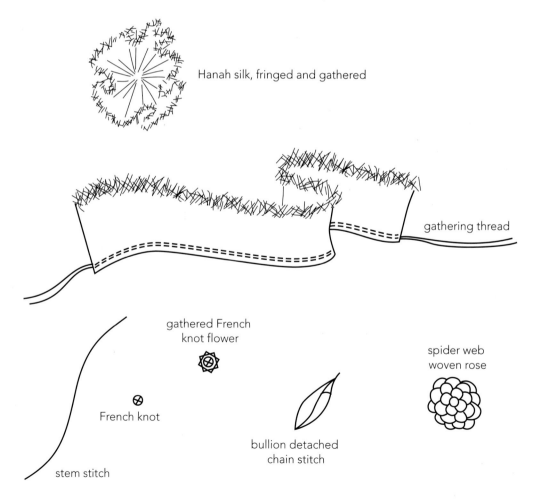

Hanah silk, fringed and gathered

gathering thread

gathered French knot flower

spider web woven rose

French knot

stem stitch

bullion detached chain stitch

30 x10 cm hand-dyed gold needle-run
   edging lace

hand-dyed guipure lace butterfly

no. 9 crewel needle for use with stranded
   threads

no. 18 chenille needle for use with silk
   ribbons

20 cm (8 in) embroidery hoop

water-erasable pen

15 cm (6 in) zipper to tone with fabric

beaded chain bag handle

Preparation

Trace the position of the major flowers and
stems, leaves etc. onto the fabric with the
water-erasable pen. If you choose a dark
fabric for the bag, similar to that shown in
the photograph, you may need to use a pen
or pencil which will show up on dark fabrics
(see Pattern Transfer). Fuse the interfacing to
the back of the fabric. Tension the fabric in
the embroidery hoop until it is drum tight.

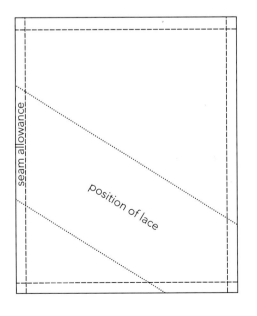

Method

Stitch the hand-dyed needle-run edging lace
diagonally into position as shown in the
diagram.

Cut the length of Hanah silk into three
even pieces. Each flower is formed by
stressing the bias-cut edge to 'fringe' the
ribbon along one edge only. This is done by
drawing the edge of the ribbon between the
thumb and forefinger, teasing and pulling
the edge of the ribbon as you go. A small
even gathering stitch is used along the
opposite edge to gather the ribbon into a
circle to form a flower. Stitch these flowers in
place. Using the seed beads and the matt
gold pearls, form the 7 bead stamens for
each flower—21 stamens in all.

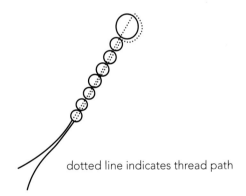

dotted line indicates thread path

Cut the hand-dyed lace leaves apart and
stitch into place among the Hanah silk
'flowers'. The lace flowers can also be stitched
into place at this point, with a matt gold
pearl bead forming the centre of each flower.
(These include the large eight-petalled flower
to lower left, and the three daisy-type flowers
to upper right and centre left.)

Work the five spider web roses using 4 mm ribbon in 'Berry' and stranded thread 745.

Work the stem stitch of each extended flower spray using 2 strands of Rajmahal 805.

The tiny roses along these stems are gathered French knot flowers, worked randomly on either side. Tiny buds are formed at the end of each stem with French knots from 4 mm silk ribbon 'Berry' and colour 75.

Leaves are worked along each stem in 4 mm silk ribbon in colour 75, using bullion detached chain stitch.

Stitch the lace butterfly into position.

Finishing

Remove any visible marks left by the water-erasable pen with a cotton bud dipped in cold water.

To make up evening bag

Trim the fabric to the required size. Sew the side seams together using a 1 cm (⅜ in) seam allowance. Press the side seams open. Square off the bottom edge of the bag 2.5 cm (1 in) in from the corner seam to create a base for the bag. Do this by pressing the side seam open. Manipulate the side seam until it lies directly over the fold at the base of the bag—sew across these layers of fabric and the side seam to create the triangle shape as shown 2.5 cm (1 in) from the point.

Turn over 1 cm (⅜ in) seam allowance at the top of the bag and hand-sew the zipper in place. If you wish to line the bag, make a similar sized bag from lining fabric and hand stitch into place. Attach self fabric loops to the top of the bag at each side seam, and then the chain handle with beads.

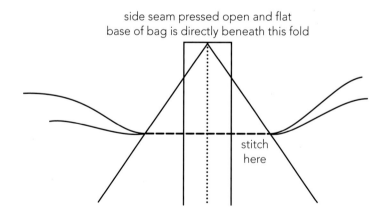

side seam pressed open and flat
base of bag is directly beneath this fold

stitch here

PROJECT 4:
'A garden for all seasons'
journal cover

PROJECT LEVEL: ADVANCED

I have used this embroidery to decorate the cover of a journal. It could also be framed or used as a floral cameo on the front of a cushion.

Stitches used

Straight stitch (thread and ribbon), stem stitch, ribbon stitch, extended ribbon stitch, extended and couched ribbon stitch, twisted ribbon stitch, French knots (thread and ribbon), bullion detached chain stitch, gathered French knot, spider web woven rose, loop stitch

Requirements

30 cm (12 in) square of pale green dupion silk

30 cm (12 in) square of iron-on interfacing (optional, but recommended)

Rajmahal stranded art silk: 29, 45, 65, 113, 521, 805

4 mm Colour Streams hand-dyed silk ribbon:

    4 m x 'Jacaranda'

    3 m x 'Purple Genie'

4 mm Glenlorin hand-dyed silk ribbon: 2 m x 'Jocelyn'

4 mm Helen Dafter silk ribbon:

    4 m x colour 32

    2 m x colour 13

    2 m x colour 1

    1 m x colour 33

    1 m x colour 21

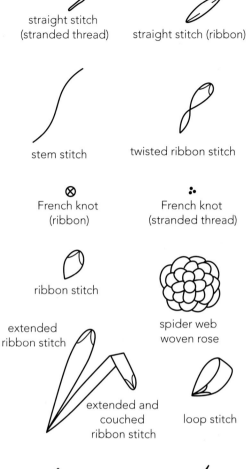

straight stitch (stranded thread)

straight stitch (ribbon)

stem stitch

twisted ribbon stitch

French knot (ribbon)

French knot (stranded thread)

ribbon stitch

spider web woven rose

extended ribbon stitch

extended and couched ribbon stitch

loop stitch

gathered French knot flower

bullion detached chain stitch

    1 m x colour 20

    1 m x colour 15

7 mm Glenlorin hand-dyed silk ribbon: 2 m x 'Jocelyn'

7 mm Helen Dafter silk ribbon:

    1 m x colour 20

    1 m x colour 72

1 black seed bead

Tracing outline
Enlarge on a
photocopier at125%

Rajmahal hand-sew metallic thread: silver

no. 9 crewel needle for use with stranded
   threads

no. 18 chenille for use with silk ribbons

25 cm (10 in) embroidery hoop

water-erasable pen

fabric paint, Decoart Americana 'Avocado'

sea sponge or bristle brush for paint
   application

Preparation

Trace the design outline and the major stems
and leaves onto the fabric with the water-
erasable pen.

   Water the paint down until it is very pale
(see Painted Backgrounds) and apply in
small amounts at a time with the sea sponge
or bristle brush. The painted background is
deeper in colour at the base of the design
and very subtle at the top. Allow the
background to dry. Fuse the interfacing to
the back of the fabric. Reapply any design
elements that may have disappeared. Tension
the fabric in the embroidery hoop until it is
drum tight.

Note Because of the crowded nature of this
embroidery, it is important to work the
components in the order listed. Some
stitches may need to be threaded beneath
existing leaves, etc. to create the dimensional
effect.

Order of work

Daffodils (4)

Leaves: 4 mm silk ribbon colours 32, 33;
   extended ribbon stitch, extended and
   couched ribbon stitch

Stems: 2 strands Rajmahal 805; stem stitch

Petals: 4 mm silk ribbon colour 13; bullion
   detached chain stitch

Trumpet: 4 mm silk ribbon colour 15;
   ribbon stitch, gathered French knot

Daffodil buds (7)

Bud: 4 mm silk ribbon colour 15; bullion
   detached chain stitch

Bud calyx: 2 strands Rajmahal 805; fly stitch,
   straight stitch

Hydrangeas (2)

Stems: 2 strands Rajmahal 521; stem stitch

Flowers: 4 mm silk ribbon 'Jacaranda';
   gathered French knot, French knot

Leaves: 7mm silk ribbon colour 72; ribbon
   stitch

Leaf detail: 2 strands Rajmahal 521; straight
   stitch

Salvia (6 spikes)

Stems: 2 strands Rajmahal 521; stem stitch

Flowers: 4 mm silk ribbon 'Purple Genie';
   gathered French knot, French knot

Flower detail: 2 strands Rajmahal 113;
   French knots

Leaves: 4 mm silk ribbon colour 20: straight
   stitch

Daisies (1 full face, 3 profile)

Stems: 2 strands Rajmahal 65; stem stitch

Centres: 2 strands Rajmahal 45; two-wrap French knot

Petals: 4 mm silk ribbon colour 1: ribbon stitch, twisted ribbon stitch

Leaves: 4 mm silk ribbon colour 21: ribbon stitch

Centifolia roses, small (2)

The centifolia roses which feature in this design are a combination flower created by using two stitches, the spider web woven rose and loop stitch.

Stems: 2 strands Rajmahal 521; stem stitch

Buds: 4 mm silk ribbon 'Jocelyn': bullion detached chain stitch

Bud detail: 2 strands Rajmahal 521: fly stitch, straight stitch

Inner petals: 4 mm silk ribbon 'Jocelyn', 2 strands Rajmahal 742; spider web woven rose

Outer petals: 4 mm silk ribbon 'Jocelyn'; loop stitch, ribbon stitch

Leaves: 4 mm silk ribbon colour 20; ribbon stitch

Leaf detail: 2 strands Rajmahal 20; straight stitch

Centifolia roses, large (2)

Stems: 2 strands Rajmahal 521; stem stitch

Inner petals: 7 mm silk ribbon 'Jocelyn'; spider web woven rose

Outer petals: 7 mm silk ribbon 'Jocelyn'; loop stitch, ribbon stitch

Leaves: 7 mm silk ribbon colour 20; ribbon stitch

Leaf detail: 2 strands Rajmahal 20; straight stitch

The signature spider web is worked in the silver metallic thread using straight stitches for the spokes first and then filling in the web with straight stitch. Sew the seed bead in place using 4 straight stitches through the bead with 1 strand Rajmahal 29, extending each side to form the eight legs.

Finishing

Remove any visible marks left by the water-erasable pen with a cotton bud dipped in cold water.

If desired, cut an oval of cardboard following the outline of the tracing design. Using spray adhesive, glue a piece of pellon or thin wadding to the front of the cardboard. Trim the dupion silk to within 2 cm (¾ in) of the cardboard oval, position it over the pellon and clip around the perimeter carefully. Glue the extra fabric to the back of the cardboard. Make a fully lined dustjacket 'cover' for a commercially available diary. Slip stitch the turned-in ends of the dust jacket, front and back, to keep it in place on the journal. Mount the oval of embroidery to the centre of the front cover using a little PVA glue. A beaded page minder, made with a few beads and a length of toning ribbon, was glued in place at the top of the journal's spine.

Stockists

Author Helen Dafter supplies patterns, books and kits for silk ribbon embroidery enthusiasts and for general embroidery requirements.

Contact details:

RMB 5430 The Ridgeway
Holgate NSW 2250
Australia
phone: +61 2 4367 7694
email: helen@helendafter.com.au
website: www.helendafter.com.au

The following are manufacturers/ distributors only; wholesale enquiries are welcome.

All threads, silk ribbons, needles, etc. are available by mail order from Helen Dafter or from your local specialty embroidery/craft store. If you have difficulty obtaining any requirements I am sure they would be able to provide the closest stockist to you.

Rajmahal (art silk threads)
182 High Street
Kangaroo Flat Victoria 3555
Australia
phone +61 3 5447 7699
email: info@rajmahal.com.au

Glenlorin (hand-dyed silk ribbons)
PO Box 974
Pennant Hills NSW 1715
Australia
phone: +61 2 9980 1993
email: glenlorin@optusnet.com.au

Colour Streams (hand-dyed silk ribbons)
5 Palm Avenue
Mullumbimby NSW 2482
Australia
phone: +61 2 6684 2577
email: colourstreams@ozemail.com.au